Q: Why did the cranberries turn so red?

A: They saw the salad dressing!

Q: What was the Pilgrims' favorite music?

A: Plymouth rock!

Q: What's the best way to eat turkey on Thanksgiving?

A: Gobble it.

Q: What key do you use the
most on Thanksgiving?

A: A tur-key!

Q: What did the turkey say
when the Pilgrim grabbed
him by the tail feathers?

A: That's the end of me!

Q: What did the turkey say
just before it was
popped into the oven?

A: I'm really stuffed.

For Mother and Father with whom
we joyously celebrate Thanksgiving;
we are thankful for you!

Connie & Peter Roop

To Wesley, Kendra, David,
Debra, and Jeff
and anyone else they bring
home for Thanksgiving.

Gwen Connelly

# LET'S CELEBRATE
# THANKSGIVING

by Connie and Peter Roop

Illustrated by Gwen Connelly

THE MILLBROOK PRESS    BROOKFIELD, CONNECTICUT

Published by The Millbrook Press, Inc.
2 Old New Milford Road
Brookfield, CT 06804

Library of Congress Cataloging-in-Publication Data
Roop, Connie.
Let's celebrate Thanksgiving / by Connie and Peter Roop; illustrated by Gwen Connelly.
p.   cm.
Summary: Includes questions and answers about the history of Thanksgiving, along
with jokes and riddles, a craft activity, and a brief look at other harvest celebrations
around the world today.
ISBN 0-7613-0973-X (lib. bdg.) — ISBN 0-7613-0429-0 (pbk.)
1. Thanksgiving Day—Juvenile literature. [1. Thanksgiving Day—Miscellanea.  2.
Questions and answers.]  I. Roop, Peter.  II. Connelly, Gwen, ill.  III. Title.
GT4975.R66   1999
394.2649—dc21   98-51380   CIP   AC

You sleep late. There is no school today. Delicious aromas fill the house. Your cousins will be arriving soon. You hurry to the kitchen for a pumpkin cookie still warm from baking. You watch a parade or football game on television. What day is it? Thanksgiving!

# WHEN WAS THE FIRST THANKSGIVING?

Native Americans held thanksgiving feasts and harvest festivals before the Pilgrims landed. The Iroquois rejoiced during their Green Corn Dance celebration. Other Indian tribes gave thanks for bountiful harvests of pumpkins, berries, corn, beans, and squash.

The first European Thanksgiving in North America was celebrated in 1580 in Newfoundland. The second was in Maine in 1607. The third was in Virginia in 1618. The Pilgrims' "first" Thanksgiving, the one we base many of our traditions on, was enjoyed in 1621 in Plymouth, Massachusetts. When the Pilgrims held their first Thanksgiving, 91 Indians joined them to give thanks.

Q: If a Pilgrim threw a pumpkin into the air, what came down?

A: Squash!

Q: How did the Pilgrims catch squirrels?

A: They climbed trees and acted like nuts.

Q: How did the Pilgrims spell mousetrap with only three letters?

A: C A T

A turkey is a funny bird
Its head goes wobble, wobble.
All it knows is just one word,
"Gobble, gobble, gobble!"

# WHO WERE THE PILGRIMS?

In the early 1600s in England, King James I did not allow any religion but his own, and people who practiced different religions were put in jail. One group of people, who were called Separatists (because they wanted to separate from the official church), decided to sail to America so they could safely worship God in their own way. They left Plymouth, England, aboard the *Mayflower* in August 1620.

Only 42 Separatists sailed on the *Mayflower*. They called themselves Saints. The other 60 passengers were coming to America to make new lives for themselves. The Saints called these companions Strangers. All these people were pilgrims—people looking for a better way of life.

# FASCINATING FACTS

In his journal, William Bradford called his group of travelers Pilgrims, but they never called themselves that.

About one-third of the people who sailed on the *Mayflower* were children under the age of 15.

The Pilgrims were not trying to get to Massachusetts. They wanted to land at the mouth of the Hudson River, where New York City is today.

The *Mayflower* traveled at a speed of 2 miles an hour. That is about 48 miles a day.

There were 15 men and boys named John on the *Mayflower*. Mary was the most popular girls' name, shared by 5 women and girls.

Wrong way!

Mary K.

Mary T.

Mary P.

Mary B.

Mary W.

John E.

John N.

John P.

John Q.

John A.

John T.

John B.

John K.

John D.

John J.

John N.

John Jr.

Johnny

# WHAT WAS THE MAYFLOWER LIKE?

The *Mayflower* was a very small wooden ship. It was 25 feet wide, about as wide as a house, and 90 feet long. That is only as long as two school buses.

Imagine 102 passengers and all their belongings crowding onto the *Mayflower*. There were also 20 sailors.

The Pilgrims packed everything they would need onto the ship. There were no stores in America where they could buy food, clothes, guns, axes, or other supplies. They filled every space with tools, dried food, clothes, furniture, seeds for planting crops, and other necessary items. They also took mirrors, knives, beads, and cloth to trade with the Indians. The animals that made the journey were two dogs, a few chickens, goats, and hogs.

The *Mayflower* set sail from Plymouth, England, in August 1620. It went right back because the seas were too rough. When the *Mayflower* set sail again, storms tossed the tiny ship about like a toy.

Many Pilgrims got seasick. Many Pilgrims were homesick.

The *Mayflower* was small and crowded. The Pilgrims slept on the decks or three to a bed. However, it was not all bad. Families prayed, played, and talked together. Even a baby was born during the voyage. His parents named him Oceanus.

During the long voyage the Pilgrim children played games, slept, and talked about what their new homes in America would be like. Sometimes they were bored and got into trouble. One boy almost blew up the *Mayflower* when he shot a gun near some kegs of gunpowder.

The Pilgrims ate salt beef, cheese, lemons, biscuits, onions, and dried beans and peas. There was no kitchen on the *Mayflower*, so most of their meals were cold. They drank beer, brandy, and, if they had to, water.

After 66 days the Pilgrims finally reached the wild shores of America. It took them several more weeks to find a place with fresh water for cooking and plenty of trees for building homes. The Pilgrims decided to name their new settlement Plymouth because that was the name of the town from which they had sailed.

# WHY DID THE PILGRIMS CELEBRATE THANKSGIVING?

The first winter in America, the Pilgrims had nothing to celebrate. They were far from home. They had little food. Of the 102 people who sailed on the *Mayflower*, 47 men, women, and children died from cold and sickness. On some days three funerals were held.

The next year, however, the Pilgrims had reason to give thanks. They had built homes. They had harvested crops of corn and barley. They had made friends with the Indians. They were much healthier.

The Pilgrims remembered a festival they used to celebrate in England to give thanks for a good harvest. They decided to have a similar harvest festival here in America. Edward Winslow, a Pilgrim, wrote this about their first Thanksgiving:

*Our harvest gotten in, our governor sent four men on a fowling, that we might after a special manner rejoice together after we had gathered the fruit of our labors. In one day these four hunters had killed enough geese, turkeys, swans, pigeons and ducks to feed the Pilgrims for a week. With all that meat and corn, the Pilgrims were ready to give thanks.*

Q: What letters did the Pilgrim boy say when he saw there was no food on the table?

A: O I C U R M T

Q: Where did the Pilgrims play cards on the *Mayflower*?

A: On the deck!

Q: What did the Pilgrims have when they caught 10 ducks?

A: A lot of quackers.

# WERE INDIANS AT THE FIRST THANKSGIVING?

The Pilgrims did not know how to survive very well in the cold, wet New England climate. The Indians showed the Pilgrims how to build good shelters to keep out the winter winds. They taught the Pilgrims how to plant corn in little mounds with three fish for fertilizer. The Indians helped the Pilgrims trap rabbits and turkeys for food. They taught the Pilgrims how to slip silently through the woods when hunting deer or bear.

Without the Indians' help, the first Pilgrims might never have survived to celebrate Thanksgiving. In thanks, the Pilgrims invited the Indians to share in their bounty. However, they were surprised when 91 Indians showed up for the feast.

Q: What did the tree say to the Pilgrim's ax?

A: You got me stumped.

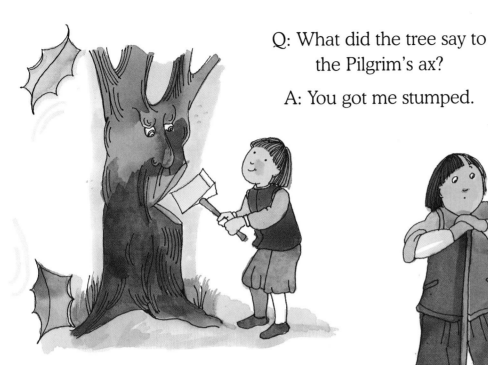

Q: How many days would it take two Pilgrims to dig half a hole?

A: None. No one can dig half a hole!

Q: When things went wrong, what could the Pilgrims always count on?

A: Their fingers!

# WHO WERE THE INDIANS WHO HELPED THE PILGRIMS?

Samoset and Squanto were the most friendly and helpful of all the Indians. Samoset first came to help the Pilgrims in March 1621, just at the end of that first terrible winter. The Pilgrims were very surprised when Samoset greeted them in English. Samoset had learned English from fishermen who fished off the Maine coast.

Squanto was the last of his tribe, the Pawtuxets. His people's village had stood where the Pilgrims built Plymouth. The Pawtuxets had all died from smallpox. White fishermen and explorers unknowingly had brought the disease with them from Europe. The Indians had never had smallpox before, and many died.

Squanto chose to live with the Pilgrims. He taught them many things: how to plant corn, how to shoot deer and trap rabbits, which plants were safe to eat, and the best ways to catch fish.

Squanto introduced the Pilgrims to Massasoit, the chief of the Wampanoags. Many Wampanoags had also died from smallpox. Massasoit and his people agreed to live in peace with the Pilgrims and to help each other. This peace lasted 55 years. Without Massasoit's help, the Pilgrims might have had to return to England. Without Massasoit and Squanto, there may never have been a first Pilgrim Thanksgiving.

# WHY DO WE EAT TURKEY AND PUMPKIN PIE ON THANKSGIVING?

No one knows exactly what the Pilgrims ate that first Thanksgiving. They probably roasted turkeys because wild turkeys were plentiful in the forests around Plymouth. We know they cooked deer because Chief Massasoit brought five deer with him to the feast. The Indians also provided cod and sea bass.

The Pilgrims made cornmeal cakes from the first corn harvest. They roasted ears of corn over open fires. They seasoned their food with wild herbs. They ate salads of watercress and leeks. Cabbage, turnips, carrots, beets, radishes, and, of course, pumpkins were shared with their Indian guests. From the nearby sea they caught lobsters, oysters, eels, and clams. The lobsters and eels were steamed in big iron pots, while the oysters and clams were baked in the hot coals.

Perhaps the Pilgrims ate the plentiful cranberries growing in the bogs around Plymouth. They did enjoy dried grapes, gooseberries, strawberries, and raspberries.

The women and children cooked all this food for the 150 Pilgrims and Indians at the first Thanksgiving. With so much food and company, the first Thanksgiving lasted three days and nights.

# WHAT DID THE PILGRIMS WEAR?

In many pictures of the Pilgrims we see them dressed in dull black and white clothes with big silver buckles. This is not true. The Pilgrims liked bright clothes of red, green, purple, yellow, and white.

The women and girls usually wore skirts, jackets, and aprons. Their favorite colors were red, blue, purple, and green. The men and older boys wore pants that went to their knees, long shirts, and vests. Boys younger than six years of age wore dresses. Neither women nor men ever wore buckles on their hats or belts. Buckles were not used until much later.

# FASCINATING FACTS

The Pilgrims called cranberries "crane" berries because when they flower they look like little cranes. They used the berries in sauces, jams, and drinks. The Indians, who called cranberries *ibimi* or bitter berry, used them to make dye for blankets and to draw out poisons from wounds.

The Indians invented popcorn. They put ears of corn in the fire and caught the hot kernels as they popped out.

If Benjamin Franklin had his way, the turkey would be the national bird instead of the eagle.

Americans eat almost 45 million turkeys at Thanksgiving.

# WHAT ELSE DID THE PILGRIMS AND INDIANS DO AT THE FIRST THANKSGIVING?

Besides eating, the Indians and Pilgrims played games and held contests at the first Thanksgiving.

The Pilgrims dressed in their shiny armor, marched like soldiers, and fired their guns. With bows and arrows, the Indians showed off their skills in hitting distant targets.

The Indians and Pilgrims competed in foot races and jumping contests. They wrestled one another. Sometimes an Indian won, sometimes a Pilgrim.

After the competitions ended, the celebration went into the night with merry songs and dancing. For three days and nights the festivities and feasting continued.

# WHY IS THANKSGIVING IN NOVEMBER?

We are not certain when the Pilgrims held the first Thanksgiving. In 1789, George Washington, America's first president, declared our first national day of Thanksgiving. President Abraham Lincoln proclaimed the last Thursday in November as a national holiday for Thanksgiving, and since 1941 it has been an official public holiday in the United States.

# DO OTHER PEOPLE CELEBRATE THANKSGIVING?

The United States and Canada both celebrate Thanksgiving, but in Canada the holiday is in October.

Many other countries have their own special thanksgiving celebrations, called harvest festivals. There are two Jewish harvest festivals. Shavuot takes place in May or June and was originally known as the Feast of the Harvest. Sukkot is the autumn harvest festival, known as the Season of Our Rejoicing.

The Hindu festival of Onam is a celebration of the harvest at the end of the rainy season, in August or September.

The Japanese have a Lantern Festival to celebrate the ripening of the rice crop.

Kwanza is a word that means "first fruits." This African-American festival was started in 1966 as a way for people to remember their African ancestors and way of life.

# PUT A TURKEY ON YOUR TABLE!

## You will need:

- Newspaper
- Paper lunch bag
- Yarn or string
- Ruler
- Brown paint
- Red, white, black, yellow, and brown construction paper for the body, and any other colors you'd like for the feathers
- Red crepe paper
- Straight pins or a stapler
- Glue stick
- Scissors

**1.** Stuff crumpled sheets of newspaper into a paper lunch bag, making a compact, round ball. Tie the top of the bag tightly with yarn or string and cut off the excess paper.

**2.** Paint the paper ball brown and allow to dry.

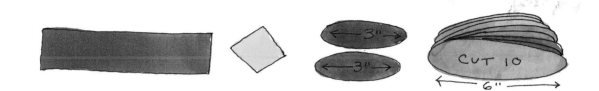

**3.** Measure and cut . . .
a strip of red construction paper 1½ inches wide and 6 inches long (head)
two ½-inch white circles (eyes)
two ¼-inch black circles (iris)
one 3-inch-long yellow diamond shape (beak)
a strip of red crepe paper ½-inch wide by 7 inches long (wattle)
two 3-inch-long brown ovals (wings)
ten 6-inch by ½-inch ovals of different colors for tail feathers

**4.** With your glue stick, paste the black circles in the center of the white circles. Paste the white circles on the red strip just below the middle, as shown. Fold the yellow diamond in half and staple or pin onto the red strip just below the eyes. Fold the red crepe paper in half and staple or pin beneath the beak.

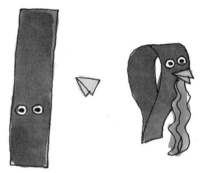

**5.** Staple the red strip of paper into a circle and pin onto the body.

**6.** Fringe the wings by cutting around the edges of the brown ovals. Glue the wings on the sides of the body.

**7.** Fringe the tail feathers by cutting into the edges. Glue or pin the feathers in a fan on the opposite side of the body from the head.

Gobble, gobble, gobble . . .

Q: Why is the number ten scared on Thanksgiving?

A: Because seven ate (eight) nine!

Q: When does Dracula eat turkey?

A: At Fangsgiving!

Q: Why couldn't the Pilgrims tell secrets on their farms?

A: The corn had ears!

Q: Name two things you can't eat for breakfast on Thanksgiving.

A: Lunch and dinner.

Q: Why can turkeys eat only a few bites at Thanksgiving?

A: Because they are so stuffed.

Q: What is the best thing to put into a pumpkin pie on Thanksgiving?

A: Your teeth!

HAPPY THANKSGIVING!